Inside Out Art

The Power of Experiential Learning in Art Education

Table of Contents

Chapter 1. Introduction

Welcome to a world where creativity meets education, where imagination rendezvous with cognition! Inside our special report, 'Inside Out Art: The Power of Experiential Learning in Art Education', we journey through the vibrant pathways of immersive artistic exploration. This unique, joyful, and profoundly enriching approach is revolutionizing the landscape of art education. Come along as we dive deep into rich stories of experiential learning projects, explore expert opinions, witness firsthand accounts from educators and learners alike, and see this groundbreaking methodology in illuminating action. Whether you're an educator seeking to breathe new life into your teaching techniques, or simply an enthusiast hungry for fresh perspectives, this special report is your key to unlock the canvas of experiential art education. From canvas to classroom, the art of learning is being reimagined - and it's a picture that's bound to captivate you!

Chapter 2. The Evolution of Art Education: A Historical Perspective

Understanding the evolution of art education is to venture into a rich tapestry of ideas, philosophies, societal shifts, and technological advancements stretching back millennia. Glancing through the lens of history provides a valuable framework for our current understanding and helps lay the foundation for future innovations.

2.1. From Ancient Antiquity to Medieval Mastery

The chronicle of art education starts in the recesses of prehistory, where primitive man painted upon the rough canvas of cave walls. These early artistic explorations were crucial to basic communication and the expression of spiritual beliefs.

Fast forward to Ancient Greece and Rome, where art was integrated into the education of free-born males. From the drawings on papyrus to the mural frescoes in Pompeii, education and art naturally intertwined. It was an expression of aesthetics, philosophy, and social status.

Come the Middle Ages, the focus shifted towards the artisan guilds. Here, the precepts of art education were incorporated into the apprentice system - imparting expertise and style through direct practice rather than formalized instruction.

2.2. The Renaissance: Revival and Reformation

The Renaissance period ushered in a grand resurgence of art alongside the humanist movement. Art was no longer just about religion and patronage. It emerged as a scholarly discipline. The workshops of master artists like Leonardo da Vinci and Michelangelo functioned as informal art academies, where apprentices learned by doing.

This period was also when the idea of the 'Renaissance Man' flourished, embodying the belief that education should create well-rounded individuals, mastering various facets of knowledge, including art.

2.3. Enlightenment and Onwards to the 19th Century

The Enlightenment and consequent industrialization led to changes in societal structures and perspectives towards education. It was deemed necessary for everyone, not just the privileged. Art education transitioned away from the apprenticeship model towards formal instruction in dedicated schools and academies.

In Britain, the movement to include art in public education began in earnest in the mid-19th century. Out of concern that Britain might lose its competitive edge in manufacturing to France, drawing was introduced to the curriculum of all government-aided schools in 1870.

In the United States, the art education movement was initially driven by the goal of cultural refinement and bolstering industrial drawing skills. The "Picture Study Movement," introduced by picture educator Hannah Smith in the late 19th century, encouraged the use of prints of masterpieces to promote aesthetic appreciation, moral character, and disciplined behavior among students.

2.4. Early to Mid 20th Century Changes

The first half of the 20th century brought about a series of transformations. Progressive education philosophies began to influence the way art was taught, making way for student-centered and holistic approaches. Theoretical contributions from John Dewey and Maria Montessori, among others, impacted art education significantly.

Furthermore, the Bauhaus in Germany, founded by architect Walter Gropius in 1919, made a lasting imprint on art education with its radical approach, integrating art and design into the total curriculum and discarding the distinction between fine arts and applied arts.

2.5. From Modernism to Postmodernism

The mid-20th century marked the heyday of modernist art education. 'Discipline-Based Art Education (DBAE)' emerged mainly during the latter half of the 20th century in response to the need for a systematic approach to art instruction. It incorporated the study of art history, criticism, aesthetics, and production.

Then came Postmodernism, presenting a radical critique of modernist principles. It held that truth and reality are not fixed, objective entities, but constructed by individuals and cultures. In art education, these profound shifts led to a greater emphasis on personal expression, cultural studies, and critical thinking skills.

2.6. Into 21st Century: Digital and Experiential Shifts

The advent of the 21st century and the digital era brought art and technology together, broadening the potential of arts education exponentially. By incorporating technologies like Photoshop, 3D printing, digital animation, and virtual reality, art education now extends beyond traditional mediums.

Moreover, the field has also started embracing experiential learning. This pedagogical strategy champions active, participatory learning, highlighted by hands-on exercises and reflection. It's reshaping how art is taught, learned, and conceptualized - linking the creative potential of the studio to the intellectual rigor of the classroom.

Thus, we've journeyed from cave paintings to 3D printed sculptures, and from master-apprentice relationships to digital classrooms. The evolution of art education mirrors the changing perceptions of art's function in society, linking it indelibly to broader educational, philosophical, and socio-economic developments. It paves the way for the exploration of myriad exciting dimensions in the future.

Chapter 3. Defining Experiential Learning in the Arts

Experiential learning involves gaining knowledge and skills through hands-on, direct experiences, a concept that forms the bedrock of art education. To fully understand how experiential learning operates within the framework of the arts, it is essential to first comprehend its roots and the tangible benefits it brings.

3.1. Understanding Experiential Learning

Experiential learning, at its simplest definition, is learning by doing. A clear chasm away from conventional pedagogical methodologies, which often require static instruction and rote memorization, experiential learning obliges students to be active, engaged participants in their education. The idea roots itself in the work of multiple theorists and educational psychologists, among them John Dewey, Carl Rogers, and most notably, David Kolb.

Kolb's model consists of four distinct stages in cyclical procession: Concrete Experience, Reflective Observation, Abstract Conceptualization, and Active Experimentation. Experiences provide fuel for reflective thought, leading to learned concepts that further enable their application in new situations, thereby generating novel experiences and continuing the cycle. It is this cycle of learning that is particularly pertinent to the arts.

3.2. Experiential Learning and Art Education

Art is inherently experiential, with creation at its core. Art education, likewise, must embody the experiential learning cycle, stimulating learners' creativity and facilitating their practical engagement. This symbiosis involves learners entering the tangible realm of art-making, reflecting on their artwork, connecting with established concepts and applying these to produce new, meaningful creations. Thus, art becomes a dynamic learning vehicle, expanding the horizons of intellectual growth and personal accomplishment.

3.3. The Benefits of Experiential Learning in Art Education

Experiential learning in art education fosters myriad benefits - cognitively, emotionally, and socially.

1. Emphasizes Learning Through Experience: Moving beyond simple information absorption, learners gain insights gleaned through tactile involvement, observation, and personal reflection.

2. Facilitates Deep Understanding: Real-world experiences cultivate profound comprehension of artistic concepts, techniques, and their applicability.

3. Enhances Creativity and Innovation: Engaging in practical art creation tasks stimulates creative thought processes and encourages innovative thinking.

4. Strengthens Self-Expression Abilities: Art serves as a potent means of communication and self-expression. By actively engaging in artistic creation, learners develop the capability to express thoughts and emotions.

5. Cultivates Emotional Intelligence: Art can serve as an emotional outlet. The experiential learning process can help learners recognize and manage emotions.

6. Boosts Confidence: With continuous practice and constructive feedback, learners improve their skills and grow more confident in their abilities.

7. Fosters Social Skills: Group projects and interactive experiences aid the development of collaboration and communication skills.

3.4. Putting Theory into Practice: Implementing Experiential Learning in Art Education

Incorporating experiential learning principles efficiently into art education calls for clear steps and a well-plotted roadmap.

- Creation: Encourage students to explore various materials, techniques, and styles. Include painting, sculpture, digital art, mixed media, and other possibilities. Experimental creations allow learners to immerse themselves in the act of art-making.

- Reflection and Analysis: Allocate time for students to reflect on their artistic process and output, appreciating the journey as much as the final works. Promote group critique sessions, fostering a shared learning environment and building critical analysis skills.

- Linking to Theory: Following application and reflection, seamlessly link practice to theory. Incorporate discussions, readings, and lessons regarding relevant artistic concepts, styles, or notable artists, relating these back to students' work.

- Planning and Implementing New Artwork: Encourage students to apply the learned theories and concepts in planning a new piece of artwork.

- Evaluation and Feedback: Continuous evaluation and critique form an integral part of the learning cycle. Foster a supportive environment where constructive feedback is valued.

Experiential learning in art education is so much more than merely creating artwork; it's a process that demands thoughtful engagement, reflection, exploration, and repeated practice. It serves as a bridge between theory and practice, providing a balanced approach for learners to appreciate and understand the art-making process, thereby flawlessly merging cognitive and creative development.

Chapter 4. Theory Meets Practice: Key Principles of Experiential Learning

Ever since humanity discovered a language beyond spoken words—an artistic universe of color and craft—education systems have struggled with merging theoretical knowledge with artistic exploration in the realm of art education. Experiential learning, a term coined by David A. Kolb, marks a significant shift from traditional passive learning, ushering in a revolutionizing methodology deeply rooted in active participation.

It provides a breeding ground for out-of-the-box thinking, encouraging students to weave together personal experiences with analytical and problem-solving skills. With immersive experiences in realistic situations, learners don't just grasp knowledge—they live it.

4.1. The Conceptual Framework of Experiential Learning

The theoretical underpinning of experiential learning comes from Kolb's Experiential Learning Theory (ELT), which is based on John Dewey, Kurt Lewin, and Jean Piaget's principles of experiential learning.

Kolb's ELT is typically represented as a four-stage learning cycle that suggests learning is a continuous process happening in a recursive circle—concrete experience (having an experience), reflective observation (reflecting on the experience), abstract conceptualization (learning from the experience), and active experimentation (applying what has been learned). This model emphasizes the internal cognitive processes of each learner as they move through the experiences.

The experiential learning framework assumes that learning is equivalent to personal change and growth, and that individuals learn best when they interact with the environment, absorb experiences, reflect, make sense of things, and experiment with their newly found knowledge.

4.2. Experiential Learning Strategies in Art Education

For a long time, art education comprised primarily traditional learning techniques where the teacher demonstrated methods and students replicated them. However, experiential learning believes that instead of waiting to apply theoretical knowledge to real-life situations, the process of learning and application should happen simultaneously. In an art classroom, experiential learning can materialize in a myriad of ways:

Visits to Art Galleries and Museums: These visits provide students with a hands-on learning experience denying all theory's artificial conditions. It fosters critical thinking, observation, and analysis. Students can even create their spin on the artworks they encounter, leading to a deeper understanding and appreciation of art styles and periods.

Internships, Workshops, and Art Camps: Through such programs, students apply what they learn in the classroom in a work-like environment. It allows them to gain industry insight and hands-on experience, embracing failure, and understanding iteration as part of their learning process.

Artist Studies: Particularly in higher grades, students delve deep into an established artist's works for an extended period. It isn't about imitating the style, but gaining a deeper understanding of the thought process and technique behind the work.

Classroom Collaboration: Collaborative artwork can push students out of their comfort zones. It demands negotiation, problem-solving, and the application of their skills in terms of the project's requirements—emulating real-life team projects in the professional world.

4.3. The Role of the Educator

The shift toward experiential learning requires the educator to transition into new roles. No longer is the teacher a mere transmitter of information, but becomes a facilitator, a guide on the side, igniting curiosity and helping learners embark on a journey of self-discovery, reflection, and insight.

The educator's role includes thoughtful planning and creating opportunities for students to observe, question, hypothesize, interpret, and make connections. They are responsible for designing experiences where cognitive knowledge and creative application walk hand in hand.

4.4. Measuring Success in Experiential Learning

The assessment of success in experiential learning is a departure from traditional testing methods. Here, the emphasis is on the learning process rather than the final product. Feedback is ongoing, constructive, and is as much a part of the learning process as creation.

Experiential education encourages the development of a learning portfolio wherein students can reflect on their experiences, the process, the challenges faced, and the solutions they came up with. The learner's ability to link theory with practice, and to apply knowledge and skills in relevant situations, is considered more valuable than what could ever be reflected on a test.

Much like the art it seeks to impart knowledge of, experiential learning is organic, full of surprises, and resolutely human in its ability to adapt and grow. It stands in the face of traditional education structures, challenging them to innovate, and in doing so, shapes a future that is a canvas filled with vibrant colors of individuality, creativity, and independent thinking. Like all truly revolutionary concepts, experiential learning has no final form—it evolves through its practice, an ideal metaphor for a system designed to foster life-long learning. Welcome to the art of learning reimagined!

Chapter 5. Case Studies: Art Education Transformed

In this enriching exploration, we delve into experiential learning as applied to art education, taking a magnified look at compelling case studies. Gathered from diverse corners of the globe, they tell a vibrant story of transformation and fresh perspectives, each one a testament to the fruitful marriage of originality and academia.

5.1. Creating Connections: The Rainbow Bridge Project

Born in a humble community in Brazil, the Rainbow Bridge Project is an enriching journey that has brought color, joy, and learning to the children of Rio Arriba. Initially a bare, drab bridge, it soon became a canvas for local youth under the expert guidance of art educators and mentors.

The children used vibrant colors and patterns to transform the bridge, drawing from their personal experiences, dreams, and cultural heritage. This not only built personal connections with the artwork but also fostered a deeper understanding of their social context.

Moreover, the project's experiential nature helped children unveil their creativity, develop problem-solving skills, and learn project management –from conception to realization. The successful transformation of the Rainbow Bridge has since sparked a movement of similar community art projects within the region.

5.2. Shattering Stereotypes: The Heidelberg Project

In the heart of an urban neighborhood in Detroit, USA, the Heidelberg Project reimagines the realm of art education. Initiated by artist Tyree Guyton, the project encouraged local residents, especially the youth, to transform their rundown surroundings into a vibrant, outdoor art environment using found objects and brightening up decrepit buildings with paint.

The project shattered stereotypes, empowered the community, and elevated the transformative power of art. Moreover, it sparked in-depth conversations about socio-economic issues, racism, and community resilience among the learners, thereby promoting emotional intelligence and critical thinking.

The experiential nature of the Heidelberg Project offered the participants a hands-on understanding of artistic concepts and fostered a deeper personal connection with art. Today, the project is not just a beacon of community art in Detroit, but also an international symbol of the power that art and collective effort can wield.

5.3. A Taste of the Renaissance: The Recreating Masterpieces Project

The Recreating Masterpieces Project by the National Museum in Prague, Czech Republic gives students a taste of the Renaissance. Armed with modern tools and traditional techniques, they recreate some of the world's most lauded works, right from Da Vinci's 'Mona Lisa' to Vermeer's 'Girl With a Pearl Earring'.

These accurate replications require serious effort, keen attention to minute details, and a deep understanding of various art styles and techniques. The experiential learning process gives students a richer appreciation of renowned works and a unique perspective into the minds of the masters.

The project, besides honing artistic skills, nurtures critical thinking, patience, and perseverance. Participants often cited an increased love for culture, history, and artistic expression post their involvement in the project.

As we delve into these case studies, one thing becomes clear – experiential learning brings an enriched perspective and a customer approach to education, transforming conventional pedagogies. By addressing cognitive, emotional, and physical facets of learning, it fosters a comprehensive growth and an enduring connection with the subject matter.

Indeed, when classrooms and canvases blend, the result is a transformative education that celebrates creativity, evokes curiosity, and inspires lifelong learning. And in the timeless words of Picasso, "Every child is an artist. The problem is how to remain an artist once we grow up." Perhaps, the solution lies in innovative education systems that blend artistry and academia elegantly, like the experiential learning in art education.

Chapter 6. The Role of the Educator in Experiential Art Learning

Educators in art education play an integral part in the experiential learning process, acting not just as mere conduits of knowledge but as facilitators, counselors, and innovators. They offer guidance, spark creativity, foster a conducive learning environment, and direct learners towards making conducive evaluations and reflections.

6.1. The Facilitator's Role

As facilitators, educators create a supportive context for learning, ensuring students feel safe and free to explore and express their creativity. In experiential art education, the traditional teacher's role shifts from a provider of knowledge to an advisor, aiding learners in the discovery and learning process.

The facilitator role requires a teacher to understand students' interests, strengths, and aspirations, helping them connect with art on a personal level. It involves guiding students to link past experiences, knowledge, and skills to their artistic creations. To fulfill this role, the educator often designs a variety of learning activities and opportunities for learners to engage with artistic materials and concepts.

6.2. Anatomy of Risk in Learning

Teaching art allows educators to place learners in situations where their comfort zones are challenged. They foster a culture of risk-taking, where learners are encouraged to experiment and explore unchartered territory. In this endeavor, the educators delineate the difference between 'productive' risk and 'destructive' risk, teaching students to recognize and appreciate the nuances therein.

Educators also ensure that they create an atmosphere that allows room for missteps and failure. Mistakes are positioned not as setbacks but as avenues for further learning and investigation, allowing students to appreciate the process of creation as much as the end result.

6.3. Supporting Emotional Exploration

Art is an innately emotional process. Experiential art learning helps students grasp that their emotions are an integral part of their creative journey. Educators play a significant role in encouraging emotional exploration and building emotional intelligence. They support students in expressing emotions through their artwork, facilitating self-awareness, self-management, and self-confidence.

Educators also work to develop students' empathy and societal sensitivity through art. They guide learners through artistic examination of global topics, social issues, and diverse cultures, teaching them to recognize their feelings about these themes and to convey them lucidly in their artwork.

6.4. Collaborative Learning

Collaborative learning in art education is an opportunity for students to learn from each other, co-create, and experience the value of teamwork. Educators initiate and manage collaborative projects, teaching students to respect other perspectives, make compromises, and manage conflicts constructively.

Art-based group exercises circle around shared goals and collective creation. This experience provides opportunity for enhancing social skills, negotiating abilities, and problem-solving competence. Importantly, collaborative learning also helps youth develop a healthy ability to give and receive criticism, an essential trait for any individual stepping into the creative arena.

6.5. Reflection, Evaluation and Feedback

In experiential art education, reflection, evaluation, and feedback are integral. Educators guide learners in evaluating their creative work, giving students tools to critique their creations objectively and constructively.

Reflection in this context is a two-fold process. On one side, students reflect inwards, critically apprehending their artistic choices and evaluating how they relate to their personal growth and learning. On the other side, they learn to reflect on the perception of their work from an external viewpoint.

Feedback is another tool educators use to facilitate learning. Effective feedback should be clear, detailed, and purposeful, helping students identify areas of improvement, comprehend their strength areas, and spur ongoing learning.

6.6. The Virtue of Patience

In a world of instant gratification, the art education process imparts the essential life skill of patience. Creating artwork requires time, effort, and repetition. Educators design assignments that call for students to persist, revise, and invest time in their creations, nudging them towards appreciation of the process rather than just the end-result.

To engender patience, educators themselves demonstrate patience, giving learners enough time to explore, create, and reassess their art. This approach ensures that students aren't rushed into producing a finished art piece, but are given the flexibility to explore, experiment, and progress at their pace.

In conclusion, the role of educators in experiential art learning is vast and dynamic. Where traditional modes of teaching see educators as mere vessels for information transfer, this groundbreaking approach positions them as game-changers, revolutionizing the educational landscape through immersive, interactive, and introspective techniques that go beyond traditional learning.

Through the roles of facilitator, risk manager, emotional advisor, collaborative guide and reflective partner, educators in experiential art learning shape artists who are not only skilled, but also socially responsible, emotionally intelligent, patient, and self-aware. The canvas of education stretches beyond classroom walls in this novel approach, transforming art education with nuance, depth, and boundless imagination.

Chapter 7. From Theory to Canvas: Student Perspectives on Experiential Learning

Art education has long been a picture of rigidity, its permanance evoking memorization over immersion. Nevertheless, the introduction of experiential learning shifts our perspective from passive viewing to active creation, opening up the artistic mind to embracing nuances otherwise overlooked.

7.1. Embracing the New Norm: Experiential Learning

The conventional methods of a structured curriculum and typical lectures have relentlessly confined creativity. Experiential learning, however, positions students to be the leaders of their educational journey. Theoretical discussions and book-learning may acquaint one with concepts, but it's the hands-on experience that breathes life into these forms. Thus, the shift to this type of learning, in which knowledge is constructed from personal experience, has led to profound transformations in art education. By immersing themselves in the artistic process, students learn to synthesize information, make decisions, and solve problems—skills critical not only to art but to life as well.

7.2. Walking the Path: Student Experiences

Indeed, the feedback from the students is unanimously positive. They express a marked enrichment in their learning, the traditional approach in stark contrast to the fresh, dynamic, and immersive nature of experiential learning. Paints blending together are no longer just a sight; they represent the amalgamation of ideas and perspectives. Each stroke, shade, and line becomes an extension of the student's internal thought processes, fostering self-awareness and personal growth, transforming the canvas into a looking-glass perpetually turned inward.

7.3. Seeing Beyond the Brush: A Focus on Process

Unlike traditional art education, experiential learning places emphasis on the process over the final product. In this context, each brush stroke, each line drawn, and each color selected invites learners to engage in self-reflection, cognitive processing, and decision-making. Each interaction with the art materials enriches the creative process, enabling students to transform their understanding of theory into practice.

7.4. The Canvas as Self-Expression

Through experiential learning in art, students found that the canvas was more than just a tool; it became a vessel for self-expression and dialogue. By creating art, they could convey complex emotions, express unheard thoughts, and evoke stimulating discussions. This revelation has caused a paradigm shift "from theory to canvas," proving that art is not purely aesthetic; instead, it can be a potent channel for communication and self-discovery.

7.5. The Pedagogical Shift: The Teachers' Participation

Interestingly, teachers echo their student's responses. Adding experiential learning to their toolkit has invigorated their teaching experience. It's not just about imparting knowledge; it's about facilitating the discovery, creation, and transformation of knowledge. The fusion of theory and the actual artistic process in the classroom has actively broken the monotony of the traditional teaching approach, marking a significant pedagogical shift.

7.6. Implications: Teaching and Learning Reimagined

By bringing experiences into the learning process, art education has transformed from a passive, teacher-centered activity into a collaborative, student-centered endeavor. This shift does not undermine the importance of theory, but rather enhances it with the authenticity of personal experience. The application of theories to an active creative process results in a more profound understanding, illustrating the efficacy of experiential learning.

In conclusion, the experiential approach in art education has culminated in resounding positivity. It captures the full spectrum of artistic exploration, from cognitive learning to emotional expression, fostering an all-around growth in the students and a deeper appreciation for art. The leap from theory to canvas is no longer a daunting one but an exhilarating plunge into a vibrant pool of personal exploration and discovery. Indeed, experiential learning has rendered the canvas a personal landscape, ever-evolving, dynamic, and immensely enriching.

Chapter 8. Impact Assessment: Analyzing the Benefits of Experiential Art Education

Experiential art education, a dynamic blend of creativity and hands-on learning pathways, is making waves as a groundbreaking pedagogic model. Leveraging a wide array of interactive techniques, this approach conceives art not just as an aesthetic discipline, but as a multi-dimensional platform for critical thinking, innovation, and socio-emotional development. The following sections closely examine the noteworthy benefits of experiential art education and their far-reaching implications in the modern educational narrative.

8.1. The Social Dimension of Experiential Art Education

The captivating echo of experiential learning in art education extends far beyond the individual learner. It advocates for an approach that celebrates diversity, fostering an inclusive environment that encourages collaboration, cultural understanding, and social cohesion. Experiential art projects often thrive on cooperative team efforts. The canvas, thus, becomes a communal space, a 'melting pot' of ideas where learners can express their perspectives, negotiate solutions, and build relationships. Art educators attest to the significant improvement in interpersonal communication and social skills among students immersed in such vibrant, collective projects.

8.2. Cognitive Development through Artistic Engagement

Art is not just for the eyes; it stimulates our minds as well. Experiential art education turns the learning process into an immersive cognitive journey, nurturing critical thinking, problem-solving abilities, and innovative ideas. By engaging with art through hands-on experiments, students learn to observe closely, draw connections, and perceive patterns or underlying concepts that may not be immediately apparent. This active exploration also promotes the development of spatial thinking and visual literacy skills, equipping learners to better appreciate the aesthetic and symbolic nuances in art.

8.3. Emotional Maturity and Resilience

Art has long been acknowledged as a powerful medium of emotional expression and resilience-building. Experiential art education taps into this potential, by opening channels for students to express their emotional states boldly and build resilience in safe, supportive environments. Artistic creations allow students to 'see' and 'feel' their emotions, fostering self-awareness, empathy, and emotional intelligence. Teachers have even reported improvements in student behavior, mood, and overall wellness, with reductions in stress and anxiety levels.

8.4. Bringing Curricula to Life

Experiential art education bridges the gap between theoretical concepts and real-world application. Integration of art into other subjects—such as history, science, or mathematics—allows teachers to waylay monotony, rendering even complex ideas relatable and exciting. Let's take the example of a history lesson; students might paint scenes from different eras, embody characters from past periods in a skit, or build miniature models of correlating architectural styles. Through these projects that seamlessly merge creativity and academia, experiential art education turns each lesson into an unforgettable narrative.

8.5. Assessing the Impact: Quantitative and Qualitative Measures

While the benefits discussed thus far are primarily narrative, one might question: What actual impact does experiential art education have? Can we assess this impact? The answer is - we can, and we must. A balanced assessment of experiential art education interventions employs a blend of quantitative and qualitative measures, capturing both objective achievement (e.g., grades, attendance records) and subjective experiences (e.g., student self-reports, classroom observations).

For instance, standardized assessments can capture improvements in subject comprehension, analytical skills, or other targeted outcomes. On the other hand, self-reports or interviews can provide insights into learners' emotional states, confidence levels, or attitudes towards learning. To explore teacher perspectives, in-depth interviews can shed light on their experiences, challenges, and perceived outcomes of the implemented techniques.

8.6. The Ripple Effect: Beyond the Classroom

The striking benefits of experiential art education are not confined to the classroom; they ripple outward, influencing overall educational policies, societal attitudes towards art, and even global conversations about learning and development.

On one hand, policy-makers are starting to recognize the potential of experiential art in shaping comprehensive, student-centric curricula and pedagogies. It brings about an overdue shift from rote-learning to creativity-infused education systems. On the other hand, it redefines societal perceptions about art, revealing it as a highly enriching, dimensional field that fosters intellectual, emotional, and social abilities. Most notably, it's causing an international stir in educational discourse, inspiring educators worldwide to reimagine their instructional methodologies.

In conclusion, the impact of experiential art education is transformative, boosting learner outcomes, spurring emotional well-being, enhancing social cohesion, and promoting innovative thinking, with long-lasting effects that permeate the entire educational landscape. By combining art and experiential learning, education takes on a deeper, more vibrant role - it becomes a creative journey that celebrates individuality, diversity, and mutual respect. As the colors of this innovative approach fill the canvas of education, we look forward to an effervescent panorama of engaging, inclusive, and insightful learning experiences.

Chapter 9. Challenges and Opportunities: Future Outlook for Experiential Learning in Art Education

As we boldly stride into the brave, new frontiers of innovative pedagogy, we must take a moment to exhale and examine the dual faces of progress. On one side, we have the dazzling spectrum of opportunities presented by experiential learning in art education. On the other, we grapple with distinct challenges along this trailblazing journey.

9.1. Illuminating the Opportunities

Deep within the recesses of experiential learning lie myriad opportunities waiting to be unlocked. A shift from conventional art education methods to experiential techniques liberates learners from the confines of rigid structures. By immersing students in art-making and galvanizing creativity, these hands-on approaches can foster a profound sense of understanding and artistic intuition.

Firstly, experiential art education tends to facilitate better retention of knowledge. Concrete experiences can be instrumental in creating memorable learnings, the imprints of which are likely to last far longer than memories formed from textbook-based information. This hands-on, project-based approach can therefore be effective in embedding deep understanding and lifelong learning.

Secondly, it fosters development of higher-order cognitive skills. Engaging in art-based experiences can spark critical thinking, problem-solving abilities and boost overall creativity. Experiential art education can, therefore, serve as a catalyst for cognitive growth.

Thirdly, it proffers an inclusive learning environment. Replacing 'one-size-fits-all' models, experiential learning allows each learner to interpret and respond to artistic stimuli uniquely, making it adaptable and highly inclusive.

Additionally, activating the elements of creative play can fuel happiness and wellbeing in learners. Hands-on art-making activities often mirror playful, enjoyable experiences which can imbue a general sense of joy and satisfaction, leading to an enhancement in mental wellbeing.

9.2. Surfacing the Challenges

While the potential advantages are numerous, the path to adopting experiential learning methodology within art education isn't without its fair share of challenges.

Firstly, the transition from standard modes of education – which emphasize more on rote learning – to a more complex, experiential framework can seem intimidating. With no concrete right or wrong answers, the ambiguity intrinsic to experiential learning might be daunting for educators and learners alike.

Secondly, art educators might face resistance to change from key stakeholders – school administrators, policymakers, and even parents may be hesitant. This is particularly true where traditional educational paradigms and testing systems are ingrained.

Thirdly, implementation of experiential art education requires considerable resources, both in terms of time and materials. Planning, organizing and orchestrating such activities demands significant investment from educators.

Lastly, measuring and grading experiential learning outcomes might pose a unique challenge. Due to its largely qualitative nature, assessing the progress might not always be straightforward.

9.3. Future Outlook and Pathways Forward

Despite the challenges, the future outlook for experiential learning in art education is radiant with promise. As pedagogical paradigms continue evolving, adaptation and transformation become necessary hallmarks on the road to successful learning.

Greater emphasis on personalized learning and integrative approaches warrants more widespread adoption of experiential learning techniques in the art education sphere. Progressive teaching strategies, in which art is used as an active means to learn, are being considered as viable and necessary pedagogical shifts.

Moreover, technology is playing a key role in reshaping the contours of art education. Applications of augmented reality, virtual reality, mixed reality and other immersive technologies could potentially amplify experiential learning instances, offering unparalleled learning experiences that are more accessible, affordable, and customized.

Another transformative pathway is the growing acceptance of art as central to STEAM (Science, Technology, Engineering, Art, and Mathematics) education. Integrated experiences that bind art and other subjects together suggest a promising future for art education, where art is no longer seen as auxiliary but as integral to the entire learning process.

Summing up, experiential learning in art education is teetering on the brink of inspiring transformation. With astonishing technologies at our disposal and shifting pedagogic focus towards learner-centric techniques, we are on the precipice of an art education revolution. We must confront challenges head-on, turn obstacles into oportunites, and reimagine arts learning paradigms for the next wave of artistic learners.

Chapter 10. Global Perspective: Experiential Learning in Art Education Around the World

Now, let us step into the vibrant banquet that unfolds as we traverse from continent to continent, exploring the adoption and impact of experiential learning in art education. In each corner of the globe, this new discovery is unearthing ingenious forms of learning, where imagination meets information, where creativity encounters cognition.

10.1. North America: A Pioneer in Experiential Learning

In North America, the incorporation of participatory learning styles in art education landscapes has redefined traditional practices. Within the United States, art museums have long harbored rich resources for pedagogy, transcending beyond mere exhibits and transforming into a hub of sensory, hands-on experiences.

Efforts like the Museum of Modern Art's (MoMA) Art Labs ensure that learners engage with and forge artworks personally rather than receive external interpretations exclusively. Similarly, the Detroit Institute of Arts' interpretive strategies incorporate visual thinking strategies, inquiry-based discussions, and tactile experiences. These alterations have shown promising results, with students exhibiting enhanced observational, interpretive, evidentiary, and comparative competencies.

10.2. Europe: The Old World Embracing the New Approach

Europe, with its deep-rooted legacy in arts and culture, has also enthusiastically adapted to the experiential teaching approach in art education. Vienna's Albertina Museum has rehearsed immersive, hands-on workshops, and Germany's Bauhaus has ventured into a futuristic pedagogical model combining crafts and fine arts.

In the United Kingdom, movements such as Arts Award and Artis have championed this shift in philosophy, promoting creative learning environments where students not only look and learn but also explore, experiment, and express. There's substantial evidence suggesting these intervention methods are bolstering cognitive creativity, personal development, and inculcating a proclivity for arts amongst students.

10.3. Asia: Tradition Transcends into Modernity

In the vast landscapes of Asia, experiential learning in art education models are blooming spectacularly. In Japan, for example, the philosophy of "iken" (experiential learning) has seamlessly blended with art curriculum. Japanese classrooms are bustling with 'Manabi', not merely a learning process, but a quest to explore life and self through arts.

China, too, is veering towards experiential instruction, encouraging student-driven projects, while India is intertwining traditional artforms with experiential learning, creating artistic curriculum that mirrors the country's rich heritage and cultivates creativity.

10.4. Africa: A Continent of Rising Opportunities

Africa, while traditionally not having a developed institutional art education system, is witnessing the burgeoning of experiential pedagogy. In regions such as Kenya and South Africa, art hubs are sprawling up, organizing interactive workshops and collaborative art projects emphasizing creation over rote learning. UNESCO's Arts Education Program in Africa has championed these movements, unlocking cultural dialogues and empowering communities.

10.5. South America: A Carnival of Culturally-Rich Experiences

Exemplifying diversity, South America has funneled its rich cultural heritage towards designing uniquely immersive art education initiatives. Brazil's Museu do Futebol provides visitors with sensory experiences, and Argentina's Proyecto 'ace has a program that involves students in real-world artistic projects.

Despite economic challenges, these programs have managed to foster creative thinking, resilience, cognitive empathy, and enhanced learning outcomes, particularly among disadvantaged communities.

Chapter 11. An Experiential Future

As this global tour culminates, it's evident that art education is embracing a metamorphosis, morphing into experiential learning hubs across the globe. The emerging trends underscore the necessity and effectiveness of this approach, one that provokes exploration and imagination, that emboldens self-expression, and that imbues learning with a creative, captivating charisma.

It's a progressive awakening, where the journey traverses beyond mere cognition, reaching towards the soul of creativity. The future indeed seems exciting, painted with myriad colors of experiential learning in art education. Whether you're an educator, student, or enthusiast, it's an invaluable pivot to acknowledge, adapt, and indeed, admire. The world over, traditional classroom walls are dissolving, only to be replaced by a boundless canvas brimming with inspiration, innovation, and immersive lessons - the dawn of experiential art education is here!

Chapter 12. Looking Forward: Strategies for Implementing Experiential Learning in Your Art Classroom

The vibrant journey through experiential art education calls for a practical roadmap. This layout of strategies for implementing experiential learning into an art classroom acts as a compass, guiding educators toward a Future where creative exploration and cognitive development sync in harmony.

12.1. Discovering Experiential Art Teaching Techniques

Art is a field that values the original and the innovative. So, while concrete tools and techniques are vital, the potential for customization is limitless. These techniques not only incorporate experiential learning in art classrooms, but also foster creativity, curiosity, and learning. It's about the process, not just the product.

1. **Live Demonstrations**: Instead of lecturing about techniques, performing live demonstrations awakens students' interest and feeds their observation skills. Real-time creation allows students to observe, absorb, and then reproduce or reinterpret what they've witnessed.

2. **Art Technique Rotation Stations**: Set up different stations showcasing a variety of techniques — painting, sculpting, printmaking, to name a few. Students rotate across these stations, tackling each with hands-on learning experiences. This boosts their creativity and broadens their artistic capabilities.

3. **Art History through Re-creation**: Deepen students' understanding of art history by involving them in re-creating iconic art pieces using their own interpretation. This results in a thorough comprehension of various eras and styles, while simultaneously honing artistic skills.

12.2. The Role of Technology

In this digital age, technology has seeped into every field, art education included. Transitioning from canvas to screen doesn't have to mean a loss of hands-on learning; when used correctly, digital tools offer new methods of engagement with art.

1. **Digital Art Platforms**: Equip students with digital art tools like Adobe Photoshop, Procreate, or Illustrator. Allow them to experiment and create effortless changes in their work.

2. **Augmented Reality Applications**: AR can transport students to different realms. Applications like Google's Tilt Brush or Arts & Culture allow students to interact with a virtual 3D canvas or take virtual art museum tours.

3. **Online Resources and Communities**: Websites, forums, or social media platforms are valuable resources students can learn from. Platforms like Behance, Instagram, or ArtStation offer a space to share their artwork and receive invaluable critiques from a global community of artists.

12.3. Creative Space, Creative Mind

The environment in which students learn can impact their artistic inclination and creativity considerably. It is essential to construct a learning area that prompts imagination.

1. **Well-Equipped Studios**: Simply put, every art classroom needs tools. From paintbrushes to pottery wheels, be sure your space is

well-stocked with the implements of creation.

2. **Display students' art**: Decorate classrooms with students' creations, fostering ownership and pride. This also contributes to a vibrant creative atmosphere.

3. **Fun and Flexible Furniture**: Using adjustable desks, chairs, and storage units can adapt to various learning activities. Comfortable, reconfigurable furniture enables space for group projects, individual work, or class discussions.

12.4. Assessment: The Reflective Feedback Loop

Rather than relying solely on the final artwork to assess learning, adopt a holistic evaluation process that includes self, peer, and teacher assessments. This encourages learners to reflect on their experiences, thus improving their understanding. In this quest, feedback serves a crucial purpose.

1. **Self-Assessment**: Entail students to self-assess and reflect on various aspects of their learning, their strengths, challenges, and areas for improvement.

2. **Peer Assessment**: Foster a learning community where students not only learn from teachers but also from each other, which includes constructive art critique sessions.

3. **Teacher Assessments**: Teacher assessments can be more structured, involving rubrics that assess students' skills, creativity, understanding of art techniques, and the ability to convey meaning.

To summarize, each strategy for implementing experiential learning in an art classroom has its own distinct stroke that contributes to a larger masterpiece. By incorporating these techniques, the art of learning becomes a canvas where students' creativity and cognition collaborate and develop. Indeed, as we move forward, the classrooms of the future are not just about teaching and remembering - they're about experiencing and creating. Experiential learning is not just a method, it is a journey, and a tour through the beautiful expanse of the mind's boundless potential.